A father's love
is a special kind
of love
that's always there
when you need it
to comfort and inspire.
It lets you go
your own way.

Ruth Langdon Morgan

Other books in the *"Language of"* Series... by

Blue Mountain Press ®

The Language of Love

The Language of Friendship

The Language of Happiness

The Language of Marriage

The Language of Teaching

The Language of Courage and Inner Strength

Thoughts to Share with a Wonderful Mother

Thoughts to Share with a Wonderful Son

Thoughts to Share with a Wonderful Daughter

It's Great to Have a Brother like You

It's Great to Have a Sister like You

The "Language of" Series...

Thoughts to Share with a
WONDERFUL
FATHER

A Collection from Blue Mountain Arts®

Blue Mountain Press ®

Boulder, Colorado

Library of Congress Catalog Card Number: 98-46834
ISBN: 0-88396-482-1

ACKNOWLEDGMENTS appear on page 48.

Manufactured in Thailand
Third Printing: August 1999

 This book is printed on recycled paper.

Library of Congress Cataloging-in-Publication Data

Thoughts to share with a wonderful father / a collection from Blue Mountain Arts.

    p.   cm.
    ISBN 0-88396-482-1 (alk. paper)
    1. Fathers--Literary collections. 2. Fatherhood--Literary
collections. I. Blue Mountain Arts (Firm)
    PN6071.F3 L36 1999
    306.874'2--dc21
                                                 98-46834
                                                 CIP
                                                   Rev.

Blue Mountain Press INC.

P.O. Box 4549, Boulder, Colorado 80306

Contents

(Authors listed in order of first appearance)

Ruth Langdon Morgan

A. Rogers

Albert Einstein

Hart Crane

Frederick W. Faber

Michele Weber

Loretta Lynn

Richard Wagner

Edward Chipman Guild

William Lyon Phelps

M. Joye

Regina Hill

Martin Greenberg, M.D.

Vincent van Gogh

Ludwig van Beethoven

Johann Wolfgang von Goethe

Craig Brannon

Washington Irving

James Russell Lowell

Edmund O'Neill

Collin McCarty

Barbara J. Hall

George Herbert

William Dean Howells

A. C. Edgerton

Chris Gallatin

Pattea Carpenter

Robert Bridges

Clarence Budington Kelland

Anne Brontë

Bill Cosby

Ellen Goodman

John Ruskin

Barrett Wendell

Mitch Townley

Jessie Adeline Phelps

Joan Baez

Mamie Dickens

Cindy Murray-Sutter

Patricia Teckelt

Linda E. Knight

Barbara Dager Kohen

Lee Iacocca

Donna Fargo

Pamela Koehlinger

Acknowledgments

This Is for You, Dad

This is for you,
for the father I love,
for the one who has cared
   all these years,
but has never heard enough
   about how much I care.

So this is for you.
For the one who has
helped me through all my childhood
   fears and failures,
and turned all that he could
   into successes and dreams.

For the man who is a
wonderful example of what
   more men should be.

For the person whose
   devotion to his family
is marked by gentle
   strength and guidance,
and whose love of life,
   sense of direction,
and down-to-earth wisdom
make more sense to me now
than nearly any other thing
   I've learned.

If you never knew how much
   I respected you, I want
      you to know it now, Dad.

And if you never knew how much
   I admire you... let me just say
   that I think you're the best father
      that any child ever had.

A. Rogers

Rejoice
with your family
in the beautiful
land of life.

Albert Einstein

My dear Father...
I feel so near to you now that
I do hope that nothing can ever
break the foundation of sincerity
that has been established beneath
our relations.

Never has anyone been kinder than you...
I want you to know that I appreciate it.

Hart Crane

There is something ultimate in a father's love,
something that cannot fail, something to be
believed against the whole world.

Frederick W. Faber

For All the Times
I Never Said,
"I Love You, Dad"

So often it may seem as if I have taken you for granted, that I never noticed all that you did for me or the sacrifices you made for my benefit. But I did notice.

I may not have said anything at the time, and I am sure that many times I really didn't appreciate you. But now that I have grown up, I realize that everything you did was because you loved me and wanted the best for me.

At a time when so many people are blaming their parents for what is wrong with them, I want to thank you for all that is good in me. You instilled it in me with each hug, scolding, understanding word, punishment, and "I love you." I just wanted to tell you that I am forever grateful, and I love you very much.

Michele Weber

I think Daddy is the main reason
why I always had respect for myself...
I knew my Daddy loved me.

If I could... I would tell him
how much I love him.

 Loretta Lynn

My sentiments remain the same...
the feeling of thanks for that grand
love of yours towards your child,
which you displayed so warmly and
so tenderly.

 Richard Wagner

Father,
the world is a happier place for having you here...

Your gift to life is a thoroughly beautiful one... you simply present yourself to those around you as one full of kindness, full of sunshine, bringing cheer and glad smiles of welcome upon the faces of all who know you. You walk quietly and warmly through life, honored and beloved by all who know you, and wherever you have been, you leave people happier and better for your having been with them.

 Edward Chipman Guild

The graduating class at Yale University voted on this question:
"What man in the world do you most admire?"

And a majority answered:
    "My father."

 William Lyon Phelps

You Are Everything
a Father Should Be

A father is a guide on the
journey to adulthood,
a teacher of morals and values.
He listens to problems
and helps to find their solutions.
He is a friend, always there
to share the good and the bad.
He is someone who gets respect
because he deserves it,
trust because he earns it,
and love because of all he is.

 M. Joye

If I Had Three Wishes...

I'd make a wish for
   your health and happiness
and your dreams coming true.
I'd wish that you would be given
   whatever your heart desires.
And after I was sure that
   all of these wishes
   were fulfilled,
I'd make one more wish for you —
the most important one of all...

I'd wish that you'd know
beyond any doubt
that I love you with all my heart,
and I'll always be here for you
no matter what.

                          Regina Hill

The Birth of a Father

The event of fatherhood is a momentous occurrence in the life cycle of a man. It inevitably triggers strong emotions — emotions that are multifaceted and often tumultuous....

I want to emphasize the importance of the father's interaction with his newborn and the impact this has on his feelings about his infant, his wife, and perhaps most significantly about himself. The process of becoming a father is a gradually unfolding phenomenon, similar to pregnancy but running on its own timetable. At times there is chaos, at times anger, and at times joy. But the process continues ever forward and in the end reaps a bountiful harvest. The birth of a child can be a process of reawakening for all fathers, increasing the breadth and depth of our view of the world.

 Martin Greenberg, M.D.

It is a strong and powerful emotion that seizes a man when he sits beside the woman he loves with a baby in the cradle near them.

Vincent van Gogh

I know of no more sacred duty than to rear and educate a child.

Ludwig van Beethoven

All fathers entertain the pious wish of seeing their own lacks overcome in their children. It is quite as though one could live for a second time and put in full use all the experiences of one's first career.

Johann Wolfgang von Goethe

How Can You Measure the Value of a Man?

The measure of a man is not found in
   the things he owns
   or what he's saved for retirement
   or even his accomplishments.

The true measure of a man is found in
   his faith and his heart.
It's found in the friends who stand by him,
the strength he displays under pressure,
the sensitivity he unashamedly expresses,
and his willingness to reveal vulnerability,
   even at the risk of being hurt.

And it's found in the truth of his words,
    the genuineness of his life,
    his unselfish actions,
    and the values he lives by.

Determine the measure of a man
    not by admiring his trophies,
    nor by comparing him to other men
      either weaker or stronger.

Determine the measure of a man
    by how much you trust him
      and believe in him,
and by how much his life enhances yours.

 Craig Brannon

It was the policy of my father
to make his children feel
that home was the happiest place
    in the world;
and I value this home feeling
as one of the choicest gifts
a parent can bestow.

                        Washington Irving

Many make the household
but only one the home.

                    James Russell Lowell

My Father's House

The walls of a house are not built of wood, brick, or stone, but of truth and loyalty....

The house is not a structure where bodies meet, but a hearthstone upon which flames mingle, separate flames of souls, which, the more perfectly they unite, the more clearly they shine and the straighter they rise toward heaven.

Your house is your fortress in a warring world, where a woman's hand buckles on your armor in the morning and soothes your fatigue and wounds at night.

The beauty of a house is harmony.

The security of a house is loyalty.

The joy of a house is love.

The plenty of a house is in children.

The comfort of a house, of a real human house, is God Himself, the same who made the stars and built the world.

Anonymous

What Every
Great Father Knows...

That how much time
    you spend with your family
is more important than
    how much money you spend
    on them.
That kids grow up faster
    than you realize;
    spend time with them now,
    and cherish every moment.
That it's more important
    to know how to fix
    a child's broken heart
than anything around the house.

Every great father knows...
That what you do
   as a father today
will be with your children
   throughout their lives.
That in any difficult time,
the best thing you can do
   is just be there.
That you have all of
   the wisdom, love, and insight
you need to help your children
   become the kind of adults
that both you and they
   will be proud of.

 Edmund O'Neill

A Father Is...

...love forever. He is caring and encouragement in every word that is spoken. A father is guidance to listen to, understanding to rely on, and happiness to share. He is a reminder that a very special person will always be there for you. A father is a big part of the best thoughts and the nicest wishes anyone could have.

...someone amazing, wonderful, and wise. He is a source of so much pride and the center of such family love. He is like a lighthouse, showing the way. He is like a harbor, enfolding you with a hug. His is the voice you want to hear when you're not sure what to do. He is the one you owe so much to, with a debt you would give anything to be able to repay.

What is a father? He is reassurance, joy, sweetness, and strength. He is the most beautiful memory and the dearest of all possible treasures. And a father is even more than all these things. Because...

a father is love forever.

 Collin McCarty

...someone who can never
be thanked enough
or shown enough appreciation
for all that he does.
Yet I've spent so little time
    doing those very things.

Barbara J. Hall

...more than
a hundred schoolmasters.

George Herbert

...the soul of our family life.

William Dean Howells

...a thoroughly human man,
    whom I admire, love and respect,
and who I hope will some day
hold the same sentiments toward me.

My greatest ambition
is to be
a "chip off the old block."

 A. C. Edgerton

A Father Is...

...one of the most
wonderful people in the world.

And though he rarely gets told that, it's true.
He's a man who, having been through childhood,
   youth, and adulthood himself,
can understand so many of the things
   his children go through in life.

He's good at providing direction and insight.
And when he does... it's all because
   his love and experience are shining through.
A father sacrifices, plans, strives, and achieves.
A father is someone who makes you believe
   in you.

A father is an essential man who never gets quite
   enough credit for the many contributions he
   makes to the family. As his father did for him,
   he will spend a lifetime trying to make
      life a little better than before.
   And he gives up some of his own dreams
      to make sure that some of yours come true.

A father is a very special man.
   He's a hand on your shoulder through
      every storm.
   His strength keeps you secure, and his love
      keeps you warm wherever you go.

And if there is any way that he can be told...
   that he is loved, cherished, and thanked,
   then think of how much it would mean to him
      ...if only he could know.

 Chris Gallatin

"Father"

Whenever I say that word,
it conjures up
such warm images for me...

The Ease
with which you went about your day,
always handling anything that happened
as if nothing mattered so much
that it could disturb your
intrinsic sense of peace.

The Strength
that you kept hidden like a secret,
letting it show only when
it was necessary
and then astounding everyone
with its power.

The Fairness
with which you treated people
in all of your endeavors,
because according to you,
<u>everyone</u> deserved it.

The Vulnerability
you showed that humbled us all,
and allowed you to cry with us
through the hard years.
The Laughter
you gave so easily,
which delighted everyone
who heard it
and left happier hearts in its wake.
The Love
that you gave so selflessly
and with so much sacrifice
to make my childhood so wonderful.

I am so proud and grateful
to have you as my father.
I love you.

 Pattea Carpenter

Father, it's your love
That safely guides me,
Always it's around me,
   night and day;
It shelters me,
   and soothes,
      but never chides me.

   Robert Bridges

He doesn't tell me
how to live;

he lives,
and lets me
watch him do it.

   Clarence Budington Kelland

If you would have your children to walk
honorable through the world, you must not
attempt to clear the stones from their
paths, but teach them to walk firmly over
them — not insist upon leading them by
the hand, but let them learn to go alone.

 Anne Brontë

Here's the whole challenge of being
a parent. Even though your kids will
consistently do the exact opposite of
what you tell them to do, you have to
keep loving them just as much. To any
question about your response to a
child's strange behavior, there really is
just one answer: to give them love.

 Bill Cosby

The Making of a Father

When he lived with them, he had been a visiting father. The sort who has his children brought in on a tray at cocktail hour and collected before dinner is served. The sort who prefers his children to come shiny-clean, cheerful and in small doses....

But things were different now. He was no longer a live-in visiting father. He had signed on the dotted line of a very formal agreement, full of clauses and subclauses, one of which read: "The father shall have reasonable visitation rights."

But now that he was officially, legally, the visiting (or visited) father, something remarkable happened. He had made his first full connections with the small people in his life....

He became the kind of parent who knew how
to braid hair and limit junk food and tuck in tired
bodies — and yell. He learned what his children
liked to eat, what they hated to wash, and where
they were likely to have left the other sneaker.
He learned that even when they'd seen each other
at their worst, they liked each other....

Sometimes he was jealous. Of men who had
custody of their children. Of live-in fathers.
He wondered why he had waited so long.

But at least he had learned. When he <u>couldn't</u>
take them for granted, he discovered that you can't
take them for granted. What he had with his children
was what they created. They had made him, at last,
a father.

Ellen Goodman

My dear papa, how shall I thank you?
It is easy to thank when
the gift of kindness is little.
It is difficult to thank
when it is great.

John Ruskin

I have had happiness enough
to make life worth living...
and I feel that I owe all this
to you, my father, and that I can
in no way repay you except by telling
you over and over again
that I realize
every day more and more
what you have done for me
and are doing for me.

 Barrett Wendell

My Father's Hands

My father's hands, when I was young,
　　would lift me in the air.
They would keep me ever sheltered
　　from the world and all its cares.
My little hands were no match for his hands
　　with all their might,
and I'd feel a calm assurance when he'd
　　squeeze my fingers tight.
My father's hands.

As I grew older, my father's hands
　　would mean even more to me.
They would toss a ball and bait a hook,
　　or even more amazingly
paint a set, nail the wood,
　　and withstand the hammer's pain —
then soften to hold his children.
His hands were never the same.
My father's hands.

Now that I have children of my own,
　　my father's hands aren't as close.
But that doesn't matter — for now, it seems,
　　I'm using them the most.
For the hands that guided and molded me
　　are now shaping my children's lives.
His hands will never lose their grip,
　　because they're being multiplied.
My father's hands.

Mitch Townley

Father

Since the first day I came to stay —
 When life and world I entered,
With loving care, you've done your share;
 Your love was on me centered.
For love so true I can't pay you;
 You watchful, loving Father!
You've worked and planned with mind and hand,
 Hoped, or prayed for me, rather.
Many a time your love sublime
 Has shone from heart thru your eyes.
As on I go thru weal or woe,
 Your great and sweet love I'll prize.
Clearly I see your love for me
 Has never yet diminished;
As part of you 'twill still be true
 Till your life-day is finished.

 Jessie Adeline Phelps

My father is the saint of the family. You
work at something until you exhaust yourself,
so that you can be good at it, and with it you
try to improve the lot of us....
You raise your children trying to teach them
decency and respect for human life.

 Joan Baez

My love for my father has never been
touched or approached by any other
love. I hold him in my heart of hearts as
a man apart from all other men, as one
apart from all other beings.

 Mamie Dickens

Along Life's Lovely Shore

Watching the waves along the shore
I envision us as we walked
and as we talked
theorizing the elements
the vastness of the universe
how it fits in time
and what we need to explore

Explore, we did, so many things
like our human history
our cultures of yore
how they may have walked
may have talked
Maybe they even picked up
a seashell or two
like me and you
Then the subject would change
once more

I found it amazing you knew so much
I looked into your eyes
and felt your touch
holding my little hand
guiding me along life's shore

Now as I walk and as I talk
with my own little one
feeling the need
to encourage my child to explore
I find it unnecessary
It was there all along
in our universe
in our human history
in all the cultures of yore

In you, in me
and in my own little one
who is a part of us, you see

We really guide each other
along life's lovely shore

 Cindy Murray-Sutter

Fathers and Daughters

When other men had daughters,
they got little princesses...
soft and sweet and cuddly,
surrounded by dolls and teddy bears.
You got a tomboy...
Your scrappy little girl took pride
in the fact that she could do anything
the boys in the neighborhood could do...

But you didn't care... you were proud of her.
You took her to baseball games and taught her
how to fish and swim and drive.
You encouraged her curiosity
    and sense of competition,
and you applauded her for trying,
    even when she didn't succeed.
Your tomboy is a woman now, and she
doesn't play ball or climb trees or run races.
But she still remembers when her father smiled
and said he was so happy to have her for a daughter,
and he told her never to put any limitations
on herself.
Thanks, Dad.

Patricia Teckelt

Fathers and Sons

In the struggles that occur
between a father and a son —
   the arguments and frustrations,
   and the stubborn independence on
   both sides of the relationship —
something deep and wonderful
begins to happen.

It is in these struggles
that the first seed of hope
for a better relationship
is planted.
   It is there…
      that acceptance and understanding
         begin to grow;
      that an everlasting friendship
         begins to develop into a love
         that's never shallow, never fake;
      and that both father and son
         are granted the freedom they need
         to be exactly who they want to be.

 Linda E. Knight

Special Memories
of You
Fill My Heart

I pulled out an old photo album the
other day and was reminded of days
gone by — of a time that seems lost
now in the rush of technology.

It was a slower time. People didn't feel
like they were running a race all the
time, or so it seems.

The photo I like best is a picture of a very young me looking up into your loving eyes. Happiness and security were spoken in that picture, along with my confidence in you as a father. It's a photo I'll treasure for always.

Thank you for being the kind of dad I could come to with my failures as well as my successes, who'd comfort me or congratulate me, who made me feel like I could do or be anything.

The memories of old are sweet, and the sanctuary you provide with your love is forever.

 Barbara Dager Kohen

The Definition of a Father

He believes in the family and in keeping it strong, close, and loving. He defines his role in life by upholding the best traditions of fatherhood, and transforming the rest in order to meet the demands of a constantly changing world.

A father welcomes and enjoys the commitment of time and effort that a family represents. He knows that it is important to show all his emotions — fear and sadness as well as strength and happiness.

He is committed to a set of values, yet he is also open to changing those beliefs when confronting new situations.

He strives quietly and often without thanks to make this world a better place for all future generations.

 Edmund O'Neill

Whenever times were tough in our family, it was my father who kept our spirits up. No matter what happened, he was always there for us. He was a philosopher, full of little sayings and homilies about the ways of the world. His favorite theme was that life has its ups and downs and that each person has to come to terms with his own share of misery. "You've got to accept a little sorrow in life," he'd tell me.... "You'll never really know what happiness is unless you have something to compare it to."

 Lee Iacocca

Dad, You're
So Good to Me

I love you so much, and I'm so lucky to have been born to you. Thank you for inspiring me to believe in my dreams. Thank you for being patient with me and allowing me to make my own mistakes; I know sometimes it isn't easy for you to sit by and watch me learn my lessons when you already know the answers. Thank you for every investment you've made in my future, for hoping with me, believing with me, and supporting my upbringing and education.

Thank you for being such a strong father image for me, such a good role model. I respect you and appreciate your strength, your judgment, and your love and compassion. If I could, I'd tell the world what an outstanding man you are, what a wonderful father you are, and what a great example you are as a father. If I could, I'd give you the highest award in the land for being the best dad in the world.

I know at times I may have disappointed you, but you've been so understanding, so good to me, and so loving. Whatever I do is okay with you. You've never disowned me for my thoughts or my actions. You care for me no matter how you feel about how I live my life. Your acceptance will always serve as the love that provides, the light that leads, and the tie that binds the heart and blood of a family. I'm so lucky, Dad. You're so good to me, and I love you more than I know how to tell you.

 Donna Fargo

You Are My Father, and You Always Will Be

Over the years,
it's been difficult for us
to understand one another,
and sometimes it has been hard
to make meaningful connections.
So much time has passed
marked by words not said,
missed opportunities,
and good intentions gone awry.
But I have always known
that you love me,
and I hope you know that
I love you, too.

Love takes many different forms.
For some people, it means
spending time together
talking, laughing, and working
alongside one another.
For some, it is a hug
or a word of praise.
For others, it is simply an
unspoken understanding that
family is forever;
it is a bond that can never be broken,
no matter where we go
or what we do.

As the years pass,
I become more and more aware
of how important that bond really is,
and although I may rarely say it,
I become more appreciative
of your role in my life.
You are my father, and you
will always be my father.
And because of that,
you will always have a profound
place in my heart.

 Pamela Koehlinger

ACKNOWLEDGMENTS

We gratefully acknowledge the permission granted by the following authors, publishers, and authors' representatives to reprint poems or excerpts from their publications.

NTC Contemporary Books, Inc. for "I think Daddy..." from LORETTA LYNN: COAL MINER'S DAUGHTER by Loretta Lynn. Copyright © 1976 by Loretta Lynn. All rights reserved. Reprinted by permission.

The Continuum Publishing Company for "The Birth of a Father" from THE BIRTH OF A FATHER by Martin Greenberg, M.D. Copyright © 1985 by Martin Greenberg, M.D. All rights reserved. Reprinted by permission.

Pattea Carpenter for "Father." Copyright © 1999 by Pattea Carpenter. All rights reserved. Reprinted by permission.

Doubleday, a division of Random House, Inc., for "Here's the whole challenge..." from FATHERHOOD by Bill Cosby. Copyright © 1986 by William H. Cosby, Jr. All rights reserved. Reprinted by permission.

The Washington Post Writers Group for "The Making of a Father" from CLOSE TO HOME by Ellen Goodman. Copyright © 1977 by The Boston Globe Newspaper Co./Washington Post Writers Group. All rights reserved. Reprinted by permission.

Mitch Townley for "My Father's Hands." Copyright © 1999 by Mitch Townley. All rights reserved. Reprinted by permission.

Diamonds & Rust Productions for "My father is..." from DAYBREAK by Joan Baez. Copyright © 1968 by Joan Baez. All rights reserved. Reprinted by permission.

Cindy Murray-Sutter for "Along Life's Lovely Shore." Copyright © 1999 by Cindy Murray-Sutter. All rights reserved. Reprinted by permission.

Patricia Teckelt for "Fathers and Daughters." Copyright © 1999 by Patricia Teckelt. All rights reserved. Reprinted by permission.

Linda E. Knight for "Fathers and Sons." Copyright © 1999 by Linda E. Knight. All rights reserved. Reprinted by permission.

Bantam, a division of Random House, Inc., for "Whenever times were tough..." from IACOCCA: AN AUTOBIOGRAPHY by Lee Iacocca. Copyright © 1984 by Lee Iacocca. All rights reserved. Reprinted by permission.

Barbara Dager Kohen for "Special Memories of You Fill My Heart." Copyright © 1999 by Barbara Dager Kohen. All rights reserved. Reprinted by permission.

PrimaDonna Entertainment Corp. for "Dad, You're So Good to Me" by Donna Fargo. Copyright © 1999 by PrimaDonna Entertainment Corp. All rights reserved. Reprinted by permission.

A careful effort has been made to trace the ownership of poems and excerpts used in this anthology in order to obtain permission to reprint copyrighted materials and give proper credit to the copyright owners. If any error or omission has occurred, it is completely inadvertent, and we would like to make corrections in future editions provided that written notification is made to the publisher:

BLUE MOUNTAIN PRESS, INC., P.O. Box 4549, Boulder, Colorado 80306.